Wacky

Basketball Facts
To Bounce Around

by Sheila Sweeny

The Ball

Many basketballs are orange. All of them are round. Each ball weighs more than one pound.

More than 9 million basketballs are sold in the United States each year. That is enough for every person in New Jersey to have a ball to bounce!

The Court

Lots of games are played on grass or dirt. But not basketball. It is played on a hard court. Can you guess why?

Basketballs bounce better on a hard surface. That is why many courts are made of wood!

Yuck!

Basketballs do not bounce well in mud. Players at the 1936 Olympics learned that the hard way. The basketball games were played on a clay tennis court. The night before the final game — *SPLASH!* Rain soaked the court.

The game was sloppy. But the U.S. team still won the gold medal!

An Old Game

Basketball is more than 100 years old. Doctor James Naismith invented it. He was a teacher.

UPI/Corbis-Bettmann

Doctor James Naismith *(left)* was a gym teacher. His students were tired of the same old games. So he made up a new one!

First, Doctor Naismith hung two peach baskets in a gym. Then he found a soccer ball. He made up rules and basketball was born.

Ouch!

Early basketball games were rough. Some players wore pads to stay safe.

The games were played inside a wire cage. It kept fans safe from flying basketballs *and* flying athletes. The players crashed into walls the way hockey players do!

Olympic Games

The world's best athletes play in the Olympics. The United States has won 11 gold medals in men's basketball. That is more than any other country.

A Team to Dream About

The United States had a special team in the 1992 Olympics. It was the first time basketball pros played for our country. The team was made up of NBA superstars. That's why it was called the "Dream Team."

Dave Black

The men's team was not the only great Olympic team in America. The U.S. women's basketball team won a gold medal at the 1996 Games. Many of the women are professional players. Would *you* like to be a pro?

The Pros

People play games for fun. But a sport can be a job, too. Some people get paid to play. They are called professionals.

NBA players earn a lot of money. Some make more than $25,000 a game!

Pros travel to many cities. In a season, a player can cover 24,000 miles. That is the distance around the Earth!

Pros like Hakeem Olajuwon make basketball exciting. (He's wearing white in this photo.) Hakeem is one of the NBA's best centers. He is a Houston Rocket.

The NBA

Great basketball players get to play in the NBA (National Basketball Association). NBA teams play in cities around the United States and in Canada.

Look at the pictures on this page. Can you match each one with an NBA team?

A New Team

One of the newest NBA teams is in Canada. It is called the Toronto Raptors. A raptor was a dinosaur. Toronto is a city in Canada. Can you find Canada on a map? It is next to the United States!

NBA Teams

Atlanta Hawks	Indiana Pacers	Phoenix Suns
Boston Celtics	Los Angeles Clippers	Portland Trail Blazers
Charlotte Hornets	Los Angeles Lakers	Sacramento Kings
Chicago Bulls	Miami Heat	San Antonio Spurs
Cleveland Cavaliers	Milwaukee Bucks	Seattle SuperSonics
Dallas Mavericks	Minnesota Timberwolves	Toronto Raptors
Denver Nuggets	New Jersey Nets	Utah Jazz
Detroit Pistons	New York Knickerbockers	Vancouver Grizzlies
Golden State Warriors	Orlando Magic	Washington Wizards
Houston Rockets	Philadelphia 76ers	

Women Stars

There are great women players, too. They play in pro leagues just for women. Sheryl Swoopes plays in the WNBA (Women's NBA). Teresa Edwards is a star player and coach in the ABL (American Basketball League).

Lisa Leslie is also a super player. She scored 101 points in the first half of a high school game. Then the other team gave up!

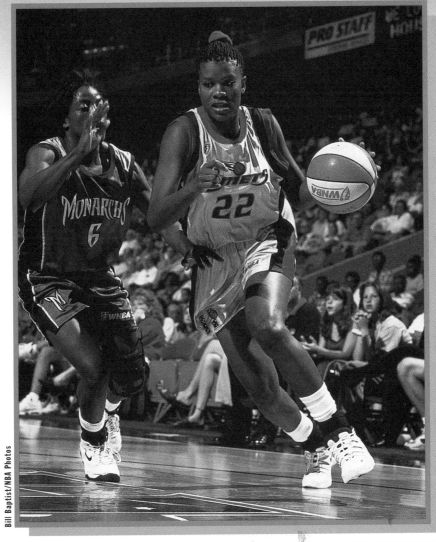

Sheryl Swoopes (number 22) plays for the Houston Comets. Some people say she was born to play basketball. Why? Her last name rhymes with hoops!

Jump!

You do not have to be a giant to jump high. But it helps! Some basketball players can jump four feet in the air. How high can you jump?

Michael Jordan is called "Air" because he jumps very high. But a red kangaroo can fly higher than Mike. Some can jump six 6 feet!

Barry Gossage/NBA Photos

It's a bird! It's a plane! It's Scottie Pippen of the Chicago Bulls! Scottie is not Superman, but he does "fly" on the court. He can soar up to four feet in the air!

A Giant Player

This is a picture of Gheorghe Muresan's hand. It is really this big!

Gheorghe is 7 feet and 7 inches tall. He is the tallest man in the NBA.

Gheorghe's hand is almost a foot long. That is a lot longer than your hand. How much? Put your hand on the picture to find out!

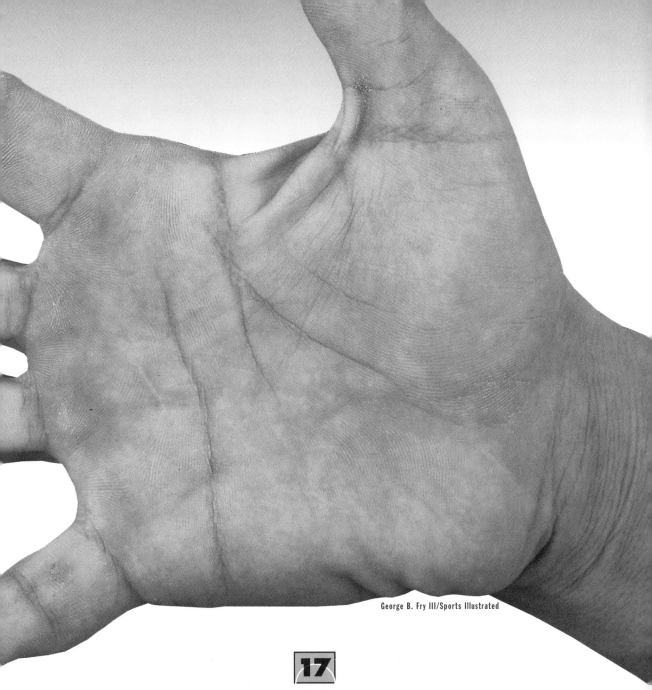

George B. Fry III/Sports Illustrated

17

A Little Player

Muggsy Bogues is the smallest man ever to play in the NBA. He is just 5 feet and 3 inches tall. Most pros are more than 6 feet tall.

One of the tallest men ever to play basketball was from the country of Libya. He was 8 feet tall. That is as tall as many doorways!

Tim O'Dell

Bigger isn't always better! Muggsy Bogues is smaller than many 14-year-olds. But he is one of the best players the Charlotte Hornets have ever had.

Hoop Talk

A basketball is not made of stone. But it is sometimes called a rock. **Rock** is a nickname for a basketball. Can you make up another nickname?

Basketball Words

Many English words have more than one meaning. Here are five words and what they mean in basketball:

To **DUNK** means to shove the ball through the basket from above.

To **DRIBBLE** means to bounce the basketball.

To **TRAVEL** means to move more than one step without bouncing the ball.

To **FOUL** means to break a rule.

To **STEAL** means to take the ball from a player on the other team.

Kevin Garnett plays for the Minnesota Timberwolves. He scores a lot of points.

What is Kevin doing in this picture? He is **dunking** the ball!

The Scoring Champ

Who plays basketball better than Michael Jordan? Nobody does!

Michael plays for the Chicago Bulls. He has been the NBA scoring leader nine times! (Each time, he scored more points than anyone else in the league.)

Michael Jordan needs a very big mailbox. He gets 2,500 fan letters each week. That's more than 100,000 a year!

Andrew D. Bernstein/NBA Photos

Michael Jordan started to wear number 23 when he was in high school. He wanted 45, but it was taken. So Michael cut 45 in half and rounded the answer to 23!

A Strange Name

Lakers seems like a strange name for a team in Los Angeles, California. There are very few lakes in the city! But there are many lakes in the state of Minnesota. The Lakers used to play there. When they moved to Los Angeles, they kept the name Lakers.

Wacky Uniforms

Today's basketball players wear tank tops and baggy shorts. That might seem a little weird to the men who played in the first pro game. They wore long tights and velvet shorts!

Indoor Rain

The San Antonio Spurs had a very soggy day in 1994. Their game began with an indoor fireworks display. It set off the sprinkler system! It rained inside for four minutes. Enough water fell to fill two swimming pools!

Think Big!

The name *Shaquille* means "little one." But there is nothing small about Shaquille O'Neal. He is a big guy and a big basketball star.

Fernando Medina/Sports Illustrated

This boy needs two hands to hold one of Shaquille O'Neal's shoes. The shoe is a size 22! You could pour four cans of soda into one of Shaq's shoes and still have room for more. Now that's big!

Shaquille O'Neal has *always* been big. He was 6 feet 5 inches tall when he was in the eighth grade! Now he is even taller. What is it like being that tall? "It's fun," says Shaq. "I love being 7-foot-1 and 310 pounds."

Go Bulls!

The Chicago Bulls are a very good team. They have won more games in the 1990s than any other NBA team.

The Bulls have Michael Jordan on their side. But the team needs *all* of its players to win games.

If 7 Chicago Bulls stood on top of one another, they would be taller than a five-story building!

Benny the Bull is a big fan of the Chicago Bulls. He goes to every game they play at home. Benny is the team's mascot. Not all mascots ride bikes. But they all like to have fun with the fans. They shake hands and act silly.

Flip for Basketball

Andrew D. Bernstein

Lots of people flip for basketball! It is one of the most popular sports in the world. People shoot hoops in more than 100 countries. More Americans play basketball than any other team sport. Do you play basketball?